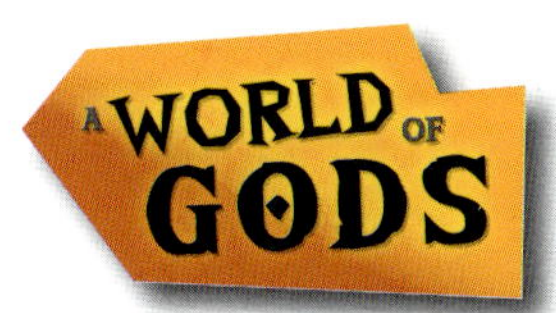

Ancient ROMAN Gods

by Eliza Nodes

Roar! Books, an imprint of Bearport Publishing by FlutterBee

Credits

All images are courtesy of Shutterstock.com, unless otherwise stated. Recurring – C_Atta, GoodStudio, Anna Timoshenko; Cover, © Gilmanshin, Vadim_N; 4–5, © Giulio Romano, Phant; 6–7, © Morphart Creation; 8–9, © Antonio Nardelli, M-SUR; 10–11, © GoodStudio, Oliver Colthart; 12–13, © public domain via Wikimedia Commons, Gilmanshin; 14–15, © GoodStudio, Livvy2020; 16–17, © CC BY 4.0 < https://creativecommons.org/licenses/by/4.0/> via Wikimedia Commons, Cetin Erdem; 18–19, © fabiano di paolo; 20–21, © onairda, public domain via Wikimedia Commons; 22–23, © Zwiebackesser; 24–25, © public domain via Wikimedia Commons; 26–27, © Scisetti Alfio, Oleg Golovnev; 28–29, © public domain via Wikimedia Commons; 30–31, © Stockbym, Gilmanshin

Bearport Publishing Company Product Development Team

Kayla Eggert, Theresa Emminizer, Kim Jones, Allison Juda, Cole Nelson, Naomi Reich, Steve Scheluchin, Tiana Tran

Library of Congress Cataloging-in-Publication Data is available at www.loc.gov or upon request from the publisher.

ISBN: 979-8-89577-855-5 (hardcover)
ISBN: 979-8-89577-859-3 (paperback)
ISBN: 979-8-89577-863-0 (ebook)

For more information, write to Bearport Publishing, 3500 American Blvd W, Suite 150, Bloomington, MN 55431. Printed in the United States of America.

CONTENTS

ANCIENT ROME

Ancient Rome was a large **empire**. It was powerful from around 625 **BCE** to the year 476.

Ancient Roman culture was heavily influenced by ancient Greece. Like the ancient Greeks, the Romans worshipped several gods.

There were 12 Roman gods. They shared similarities with Greek gods, but most had different names. Each god had their own powers.

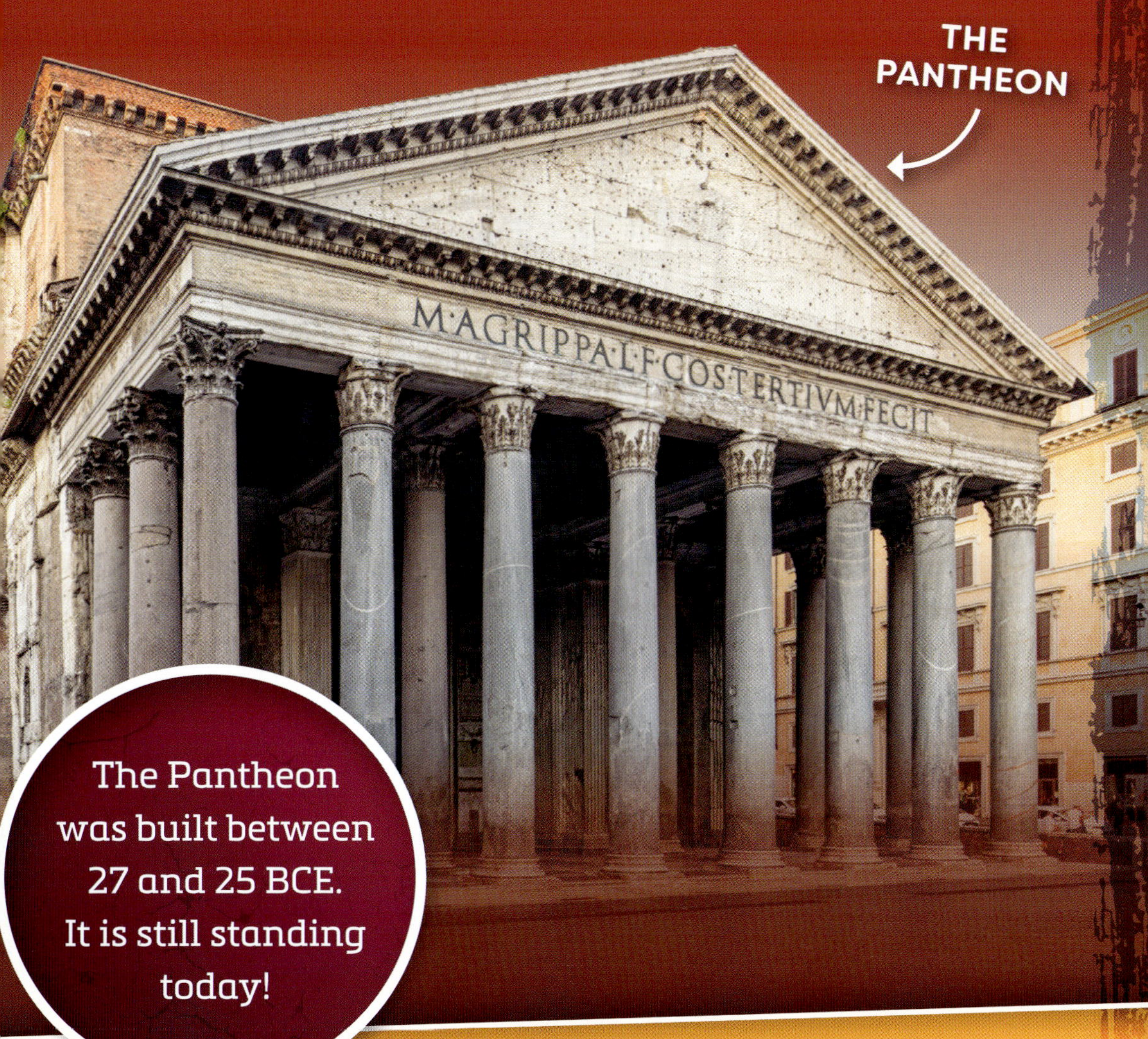

The Pantheon was built between 27 and 25 BCE. It is still standing today!

The Roman gods are sometimes referred to as the Roman pantheon. This is also the name of a temple the Romans built to honor their gods.

JUPITER

Jupiter was king of the Roman pantheon. He was the god of the sky and weather.

Jupiter is often shown holding lightning bolts. The Romans believed that anywhere lightning struck belonged to Jupiter.

Temples and shrines were places to worship the gods. Jupiter's oldest temple was on Capitoline Hill, one of the seven hills of Rome.

Humans and creatures alike came to Jupiter's temple to ask him for blessings.

JUPITER AND THE BEE

All living things sought help from Jupiter. According to Roman stories, a queen bee once came to him seeking a gift.

She was tired of other creatures stealing her honey. So, the bee asked Jupiter to give her a weapon she could use to protect her honey.

Jupiter gave her a stinger. But he did not want the queen bee to kill other creatures.

So, his gift came at a cost. The bee would die if she used her stinger. The animal faced a terrible choice. She could let others steal her honey, or she could use her stinger and die.

Romans believed that this deal with Jupiter was why bees died after they stung someone.

MINERVA

Minerva was Jupiter's daughter.

She was praised for her wisdom. Leaders sought Minerva's help in matters of war and other problems. She was also a goddess of art and a skillful **craftsperson**.

The owl became a sign of Minerva's wisdom. Owls are still seen as a sign of wisdom today.

Minerva's temple stood on Aventine Hill in Rome. It was close to the Roman halls, where craftspeople worked and sold their goods.

Ancient Roman crafts included pottery, jewelry making, and weaving.

ARACHNE THE WEAVER

Minerva considered herself to be the best weaver. One day, a human weaver named Arachne bragged that she was a better weaver than Minerva.

Arachne challenged Minerva to a weaving contest. The woman made a **tapestry** showing all the terrible things the gods had done to humans.

MINERVA

Outraged, Minerva broke Arachne's loom. This left the woman heartbroken. She thought she would never weave again.

But then, Minerva turned Arachne into a spider. As a creature with her own silk, Arachne could spend her days weaving.

APOLLO

Apollo was Jupiter's son. He had a twin sister named Diana. Apollo was the god of light, **prophecy**, and music.

One of Apollo's symbols was the lyre. This is a small stringed instrument, a bit like a harp.

LYRE

But the Romans also associated Apollo with sickness. They believed the god could spread plagues among humans.

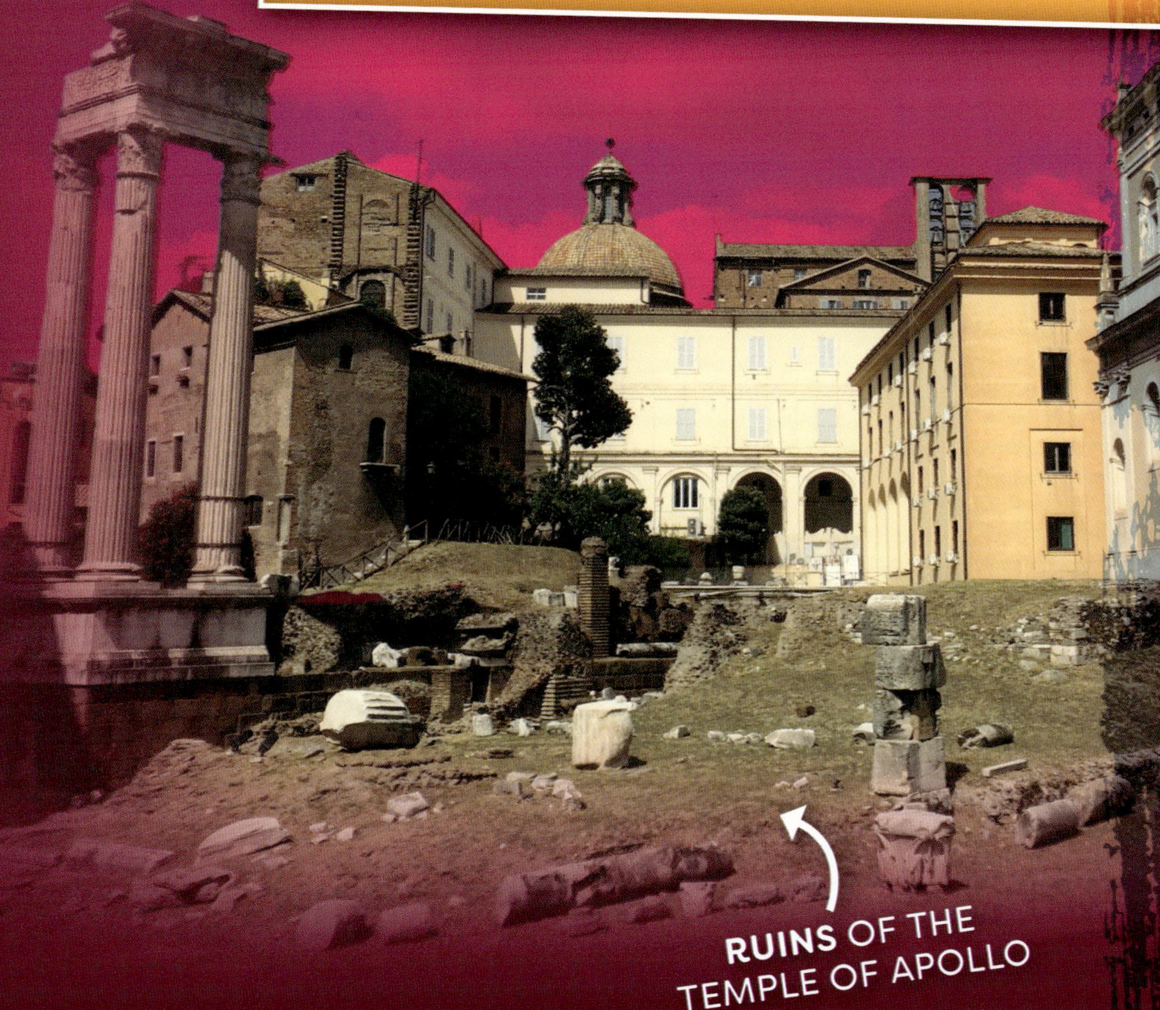

RUINS OF THE TEMPLE OF APOLLO

They also thought he had the power to take the sickness away. As one terrible plague spread, the Romans built a temple. There, they asked Apollo to free them from the illness.

APOLLO'S CHARIOT

As the god of light, Apollo was thought to bring the sun up every day. He pulled it into the sky behind a horse-drawn chariot.

One day, Apollo's human son, Phaethon, asked his father if he could drive the chariot. He believed it would prove to his friends that he was truly the god of light's son.

Apollo finally agreed to let Phaethon drive the chariot.

But Phaethon could not control his father's horses. He was thrown out of the chariot and died. After that, Apollo never rode the chariot again.

DIANA

Diana was Apollo's twin sister. The Romans believed that she protected people who were **enslaved**. Enslaved people in ancient Rome had a holiday to celebrate Diana.

Diana is often shown with a bow and arrows.

People worshipped Diana at a shrine called Diana of the Wood. The shrine stood on the shores of Lake Nemi near Rome.

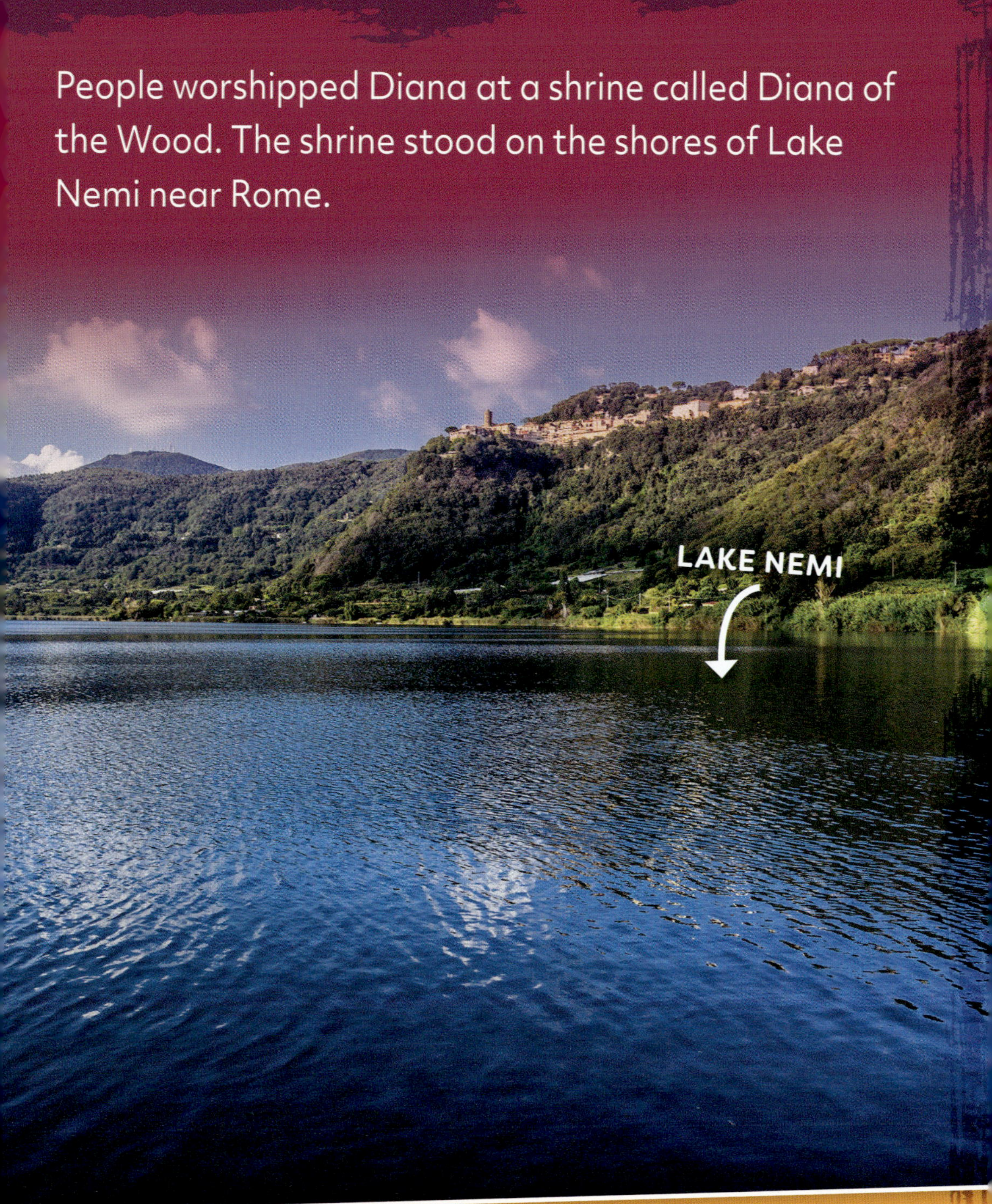

The woods were a special place for Diana. Wildlife was sacred to her.

DIANA AND ACTAEON

The stag was one of Diana's sacred animals. One day, a hunter named Actaeon and his dogs chased a stag through the woods.

As they did, Actaeon stumbled into a clearing. He saw Diana bathing in a stream.

Diana was angry with the hunter for spying on her and for chasing down one of her animals. So, she turned *him* into a stag!

A STATUE OF ACTAEON AND HIS DOGS

Not knowing that the stag was their master, Actaeon's dogs attacked. They turned on him and ate him.

MERCURY

Mercury was another one of Jupiter's sons. He was the messenger of the gods.

Jupiter often sent Mercury to give orders to others. The messenger wore winged sandals to help him move very quickly on his travels.

This god was often worshipped by merchants, who hoped for luck on their own long journeys. They went to a temple for Mercury on Aventine Hill in Rome.

Mercury's temple was built around 495 BCE.

Merchants also celebrated a festival to the god. During this celebration, they took water from Mercury's sacred well and sprinkled it on themselves.

MERCURY FREES IO

One day, Jupiter sent Mercury on a very special mission. He wanted his son to free a human woman named Io, whom the king of gods had fallen in love with.

Io had been turned into a cow by Jupiter's jealous wife, Juno. And the cow Io had been sent to a field where she was guarded by the god Argus.

But Mercury was a clever and talented musician. He went to Argus and began to play his pipes. Soon, Argus drifted off to sleep.

Argus had 100 eyes. He could see anybody coming to try and free Io.

Once Argus was fast asleep, Mercury stabbed him. Then, Mercury set his father's love free.

VENUS

The Romans thought of Venus as the mother of Rome. She was the **ancestor** of Romulus and Remus, the founders of the city.

Venus was known for her beauty. She wore a crown of myrtle flowers in her hair. Myrtle crowns were often worn at ancient Roman weddings.

A MYRTLE FLOWER

Venus was the goddess of love. She had many children with gods and humans. Cupid was her most famous child.

VENUS *(RIGHT)* **AND CUPID** *(LEFT)*

CUPID AND PSYCHE

Though Venus was beautiful, she could also be very cruel. Her jealousy sometimes got the best of her.

There was once a beautiful princess named Psyche. People worshipped Psyche, which made Venus angry. She asked Cupid for help.

Her son's arrows could make people fall in love with the first thing they saw. Venus told him to make Psyche fall in love with an ugly animal.

Instead, Cupid fell in love with Psyche! He asked her to marry him. Although Venus was angry, Jupiter allowed the marriage. Psyche became a goddess and lived forever by Cupid's side.

THE LEGENDS LIVE ON

The Roman gods and goddesses did not disappear with the fall of the Roman empire.

Their stories have inspired artwork, books, movies, and more. Though the ancient Romans are gone, their gods live on!

GLOSSARY

ancestor a person in a family who lived a long time ago

BCE before Common Era, the time before the year 1

craftsperson someone who is skilled at making things by hand

empire a large region ruled by a single person or government

enslaved made to work without being paid

loom a tool used for weaving

prophecy a statement of what will happen in the future

ruins the remains of buildings

sacred something that was important to a god

tapestry a heavy piece of fabric that has pictures woven onto it

INDEX

READ MORE

Leatherland, Noah. *Life in Ancient Rome (Baffling Behavior in the Past).* Minneapolis: Bearport Publishing, 2025.

Lynch, Seth. *Ancient Rome (Ancient Civilizations in Review).* Buffalo, NY: Enslow Publishing, 2025.

LEARN MORE ONLINE

1. Go to **FactSurfer.com** or scan the QR code below.
2. Enter "**Roman Gods**" into the search box.
3. Click on the cover of this book to see a list of websites.